Careers without College

Crime Lab
Technician

by David Heath

Consultant:

Richard R. Auge
Crime Lab Supervisor
Ramsey County Sheriff Department

CAPSTONE
HIGH/LOW BOOKS
an imprint of Capstone Press
Mankato, Minnesota

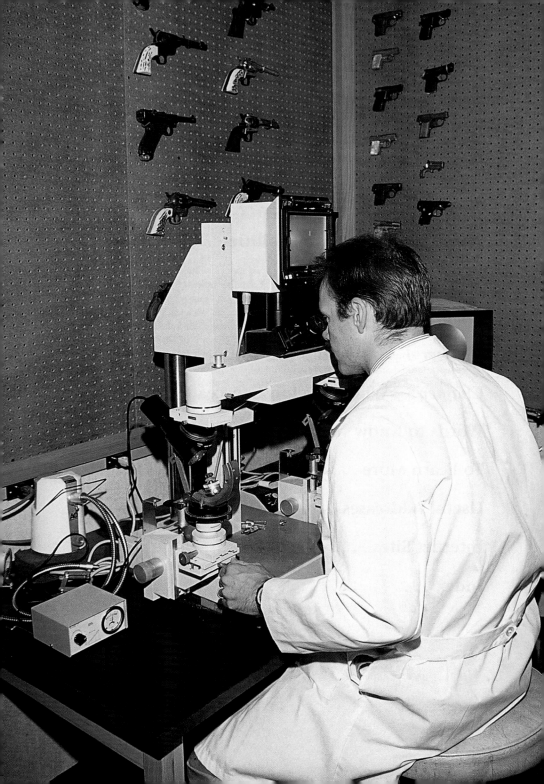

Fast Facts

Career Title_____Crime lab technician

Minimum Educational_____U.S.: associate's degree
Requirement   Canada: associate's degree

Certification Requirement_____U.S.: varies by state
                                    Canada: varies by province

Salary Range_____U.S.: $15,500 to $49,500
(U.S. Bureau of Labor Statistics and   Canada: $32,500 to $58,000
Royal Canadian Mounted Police,
late 1990s figures)   (Canadian dollars)

Job Outlook_____U.S.: average growth
(U.S. Bureau of Labor Statistics and   Canada: fair
Human Resources Development
Canada, late 1990s projections)

DOT Cluster_____Professional, technical, and
(Dictionary of Occupational Titles)   managerial occupations

DOT Number_____029.261-026

GOE Number_____02.04.01
(Guide for Occupational Exploration)

NOC_____2221
(National Occupational Classification—Canada)

Chapter 1

Job Responsibilities

Crime lab technicians play an important role in law enforcement. Crime lab technicians help law enforcement officers solve crimes. These technicians sometimes are called criminalists.

Crime lab technicians gather evidence at crime scenes. Evidence may provide information about crimes. Technicians also may help find out how auto accidents happened. For example, they may take measurements of tire marks on roads after accidents.

On the Scene

Crime lab technicians record facts at crime and accident scenes. They videotape and photograph items found at such scenes. For example, they may take photographs of broken windows, weapons, or vehicles.

Crime lab technicians photograph crime scenes.

They sometimes take photographs of crime or accident victims. These people may be injured or even dead.

Crime lab technicians collect evidence at crime and accident scenes. They put each piece of evidence into a bag. They then label the bag with that day's date and where the evidence was found. Evidence must be handled carefully.

Crime lab technicians often work with police officers. Technicians help officers and detectives gather clues about crimes.

In the Lab

Crime lab technicians study evidence at crime laboratories. Technicians do tests on evidence. For example, some crime lab technicians check weapons for fingerprints. These ridges are found on people's fingers, palms, and feet. The ridge patterns are different on each finger. Each person's fingerprints are different. Fingerprints help identify criminals and victims.

Some crime lab technicians check substances to see if they are drugs. Technicians test these substances with chemicals that identify different

Crime lab technicians test items with chemicals that identify drugs.

drugs. Sometimes scientists must do more tests on substances to prove what types of drugs they are.

Technicians must keep good records. They write reports about evidence they find. They must keep evidence in safe places. They also write reports on the tests they perform on evidence. Reports and evidence may be used in court trials.

Some crime lab technicians are experts in special areas.

Special Kinds of Technicians

There are different types of crime lab technicians. Each type of technician has special duties. These technicians are experts in their special areas. Some crime lab technicians work in several special areas.

In the United States, crime scene technicians also are known as evidence technicians. These technicians gather evidence. They are experts at examining crime scenes. They take notes about what they see. They may draw sketches, take photographs, and make videotapes.

In Canada, evidence technicians are called forensic identification specialists. These individuals are police officers in the Royal Canadian Mounted Police (RCMP) or provincial police departments. The RCMP is Canada's national police force. It also is the police force in every province and territory except Ontario and Quebec.

Fingerprint examiners check evidence for fingerprints. They use special powders, chemicals, and lights to help them see fingerprints. Fingerprint examiners take photographs of exposed fingerprints. They compare an individual's fingerprints to a fingerprint found at a crime scene or on evidence.

Fingerprint examiners work with a variety of people. For example, they may work with forensic pathologists to identify dead people by their fingerprints. Forensic pathologists are medical doctors who specialize in determining a person's cause of death.

Tire track experts examine and identify tire tracks left at crime scenes or on objects. They compare

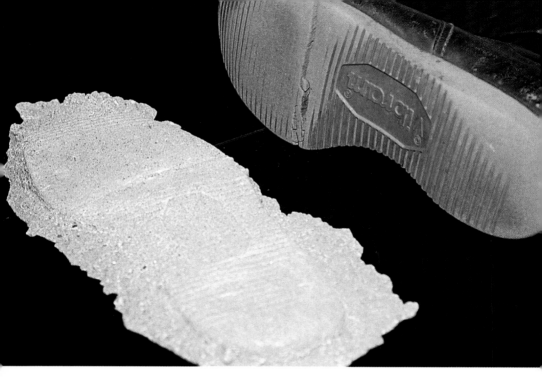

Shoeprint experts compare shoeprints to certain shoes.

these tracks to tires of certain vehicles. They want to see if these vehicles left the tracks. Tire track experts research tire tread patterns. They can tell what type of tire or vehicle leaves certain tracks.

Footwear or shoeprint experts examine shoeprints left on objects or at crime scenes. They compare the shoeprints to prints of certain shoes. They want to see what type of shoe left the prints.

Toxicology experts test for drugs and other harmful chemicals. They most commonly test blood, urine, and hair for traces of these substances. They may test victims and criminals to decide if these people used drugs.

Firearms and toolmark experts examine imprints left by guns and hard objects. Firearms experts test bullets and shells to see what kind of gun fired them. They use special microscopes to study bullets. Toolmark experts look at markings left by tools such as hammers, screwdrivers, and saws. Markings are scratches or stains on items. Toolmark experts try to decide which items match marks left at crime scenes.

Trace evidence experts examine tiny pieces of evidence from crime scenes. For example, they look for paint chips, cloth fibers, or hair. They compare this evidence to items belonging to victims and suspects. Suspects are people thought to be responsible for crimes. One goal of trace evidence experts is to determine who was present at the time of a crime.

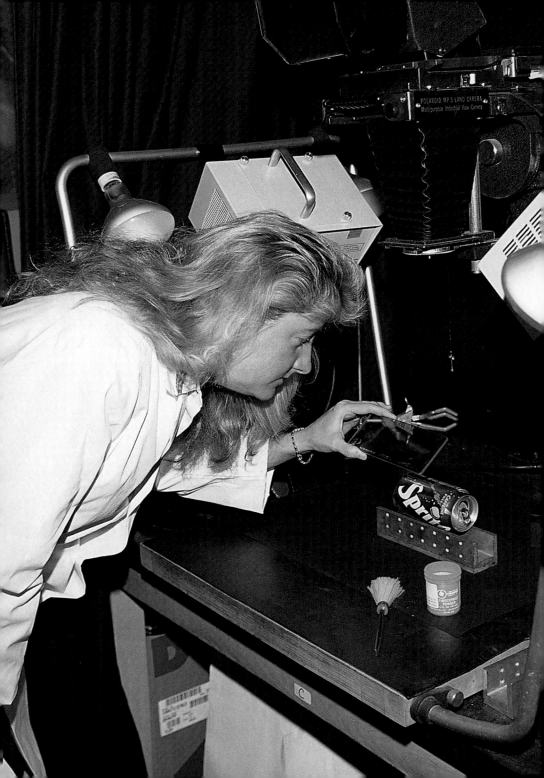

Chapter 2

What the Job Is Like

Crime lab technicians spend much of their time in laboratories. Most crime labs are small and crowded. This even is true of crime labs in many large cities.

Crime labs are filled with equipment and supplies. Tables support computers and photo equipment. Shelves contain books and folders. File cabinets store files and information about crimes. Boxes hold evidence that needs to be examined or checked.

One end of the lab might be set up for chemical tests. Chemicals can be dangerous. Crime lab technicians store and use chemicals in secure places.

Many crime labs have a darkroom. Technicians develop film and print photographs in this room.

Crime lab technicians work in laboratories equipped with equipment and supplies.

Some crime lab technicians gather evidence.

Crime labs often use computer technology. Technicians scan photographs and other images using a computer scanner. This machine makes electronic copies of photographs that can be viewed with computers. Technicians can enhance and enlarge images with computers and darkroom equipment. To enhance an image, a technician may change a color image to a black-and-white one. Images sometimes are easier to see when the color is removed.

Work Environment

Some crime lab technicians also serve as crime scene technicians. These technicians may be called to a crime scene at any time. It often is easier for technicians to understand evidence in the lab if they also view it at crime scenes.

Most small crime labs are part of local police or sheriffs departments. These labs usually are in the same building as police stations.

State governments run some large crime labs. These labs usually are located in their own buildings. The Federal Bureau of Investigation (FBI) has one of the largest and most developed crime labs in the United States. State and federal labs employ scientists. These individuals have more training than crime lab technicians. Most state labs do not employ technicians.

In Canada, most of the crime labs are operated by the RCMP. It operates six forensic labs in Canada. There also are two provincial labs in Ontario and one lab in Quebec. Forensic specialists perform most of the evidence examinations. These people have more education and training than crime lab technicians. In Canada, crime lab technicians are called forensic technologists. These individuals are civilians. The RCMP employs the most forensic technologists in Canada.

Large labs do specialized testing. These labs can handle many tests that cannot be done in smaller labs. For example, large labs may be able to test for DNA. This molecule carries the genetic code that gives living things their special features. The genetic code is commonly known as a DNA fingerprint. People can be identified through their DNA.

Large labs are better equipped to handle special testing than small labs. Large labs have more equipment. They also employ many experts. Small labs send evidence to large labs for specialized tests.

Most crime lab technicians work regular daytime hours. They usually work 40 hours each week. Sometimes technicians work more than 40 hours in a week. The extra hours are called overtime.

Crime lab technicians must finish their duties quickly and accurately.

Crime lab technicians must finish most of their duties quickly. Technicians have tight deadlines. They must finish their work in a short amount of time.

The work schedule varies for some crime lab technicians. Crime scene technicians often are on call. These technicians must come to crime scenes promptly when called. They must be able to work anytime

Crime lab technicians often testify in court.

during the day or night. They also may have to work on weekends and holidays. Sometimes technicians may have to stay on crime scenes for several days.

Personal Qualities
Crime lab technicians should have qualities that help them in their work. Technicians should be

interested in science and mathematics. Technicians often use science and mathematics to perform tests and solve crimes.

Crime lab technicians also must be careful, observant, and organized. They must keep detailed records of evidence and tests. These records must be complete and correct. Records often will be used in court trials.

Crime lab technicians also must know how to store evidence properly. Evidence often is used months or even years after technicians gather and test it.

Crime lab technicians must be willing to learn new things. Technicians must continue to study and take classes as technology changes. They also must learn new procedures. New knowledge and training help them to do their jobs better.

Crime lab technicians need good communication skills. They deal with many different people. They may need to ask these people questions. Technicians sometimes have to testify in court. They have to state facts in court in front of lawyers, juries, and judges. They must explain how they did their tests and what they discovered.

Chapter 3

Training

People prepare to be crime lab technicians through studying and training. Technicians must have a high school diploma. They also must study at colleges or technical schools after high school.

Some crime lab technicians may have an associate's degree in law enforcement or medical technology. People earn associate's degrees by completing programs of study at technical schools or colleges. People usually earn these degrees in two years. Many technical and community colleges offer associate's degrees in science, law enforcement, and mathematics. Many schools in Canada also offer similar degrees.

Some crime lab technicians earn bachelor's degrees in science. People earn bachelor's degrees

People prepare to be crime lab technicians through studying and training.

Many crime lab technicians in the United States also are law enforcement officers.

by completing courses of study at colleges or universities. People usually earn bachelor's degrees in about four years.

Many crime lab technicians in the United States are law enforcement officers. They have graduated from police academies or technical schools. They are trained to enforce laws. These people work first as police officers. They then are able to become crime lab technicians. They may take classes at schools and receive on-the-job training.

Some crime lab technicians continue their education after working as technicians for a few years. They may attend college and receive a bachelor's degree. They then may become scientists. Some technicians study sciences such as biology or chemistry. Others technicians study law enforcement.

What Crime Lab Technicians Study

Some community colleges, technical colleges, and universities offer programs for crime lab technicians. Students in these programs take classes in science and math. They learn how to use lab equipment. They learn how to work with chemicals. They learn about proper lab safety procedures. These safety steps prevent accidents in labs.

Some crime lab technicians also take courses in law enforcement. They learn how to look for evidence. They study proper ways to gather evidence and perform tests. Students who want to become police officers learn how to enforce laws. These students may learn how to use guns or other firearms.

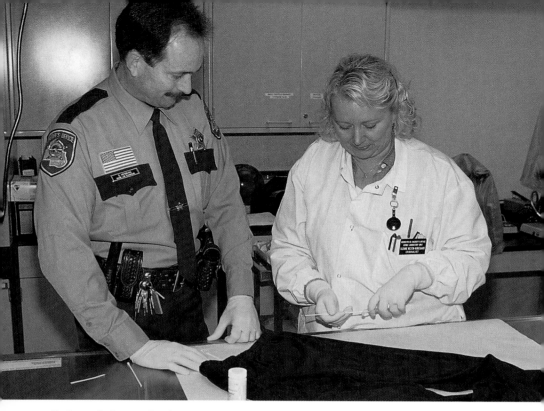

Crime lab technicians learn how to look for evidence.

Some crime lab technicians study certain subjects in addition to basic courses. For example, firearms and toolmark experts study metallurgy. This science and study of metals enables experts to understand how different metals react.

Licensing and Certification

Most crime lab technicians do not need a special license. A license is a document giving permission for a person to do something. But crime lab technicians who also are police officers need law enforcement licenses. Licensing requirements vary in each state and province.

Crime lab technicians continue to learn on the job. Technicians can earn different certificates. These certificates state that technicians are able to do certain kinds of lab work. For example, technicians who are trained to identify drugs can get a certificate in toxicology.

Crime lab technicians can become certified through a national testing program. Technicians can get certified in many areas including fingerprints, footwear, and toolmarks. Technicians pass tests to become certified in these special areas.

Employers differ in the testing requirements for crime lab technicians. Some employers require technicians to take a national test. Most of these employers also train and test technicians to certify them. Other employers do not require technicians to take a national test. These employers train and test technicians. The employees are then certified in the specialty area in which they tested.

Certified crime lab technicians are experts. Lawyers and police departments ask experts to help with special criminal cases. Many of these experts testify in court. Experts tell what information they discovered. They also tell where they found evidence and what tests they performed. People trust information from experts because of their education and experience.

Some technicians are considered certified after they testify in court. These technicians are court certified as experts in the areas in which they testified.

On-the-Job Training

Many crime labs offer on-the-job training for their technicians and scientists. In large labs, technicians may be able to specialize in areas of testing. These technicians are trained in specific areas.

Crime lab technicians learn a great deal on the job. They learn from crime lab managers and other technicians. Crime lab technicians also learn from police officers and detectives. For example,

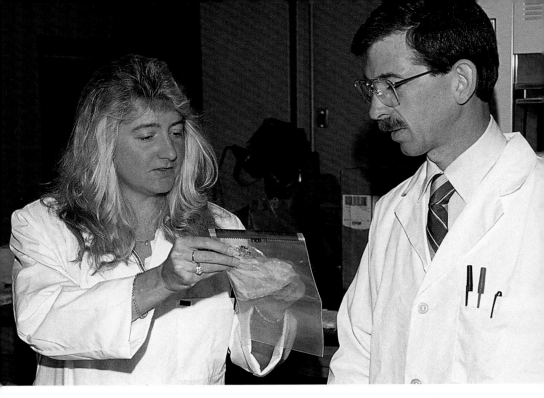

Crime lab technicians learn from others on the job.

technicians may learn different ways of testing or gathering evidence.

Crime lab technicians also learn by reading journals and trade magazines. These publications are for people in a certain work area. Publications for crime lab technicians include articles about the use of equipment and new procedures. This information

Crime lab technicians may need art skills.

helps technicians learn new and better ways to perform their jobs.

Crime lab technicians receive education in other ways as well. Technicians go to meetings about their profession. They discuss their work with other technicians and scientists at these meetings. They may learn about new equipment and procedures.

What Students Can Do Now

Students who want to be crime lab technicians can prepare while still in high school. They should study science and math. Students should know how to work in labs. Crime lab technicians need to take careful measurements. They also need to do many scientific and mathematical tests.

English and communication classes help students who want to be crime lab technicians. Technicians write many reports. They need to understand rules of grammar, spelling, and punctuation. They need to know how to present information in court cases. They also need to know how to speak well with police officers, witnesses, and fellow technicians.

Students also can benefit from photography and art classes. Technicians take photographs of crime scenes. They also take photographs of weapons and other evidence. Some technicians make drawings. They sketch pictures of crime scenes.

Chapter 4

Salary and Job Outlook

Crime lab technicians' salaries vary. Beginning technicians earn less than experienced technicians. Crime lab technicians in large cities usually earn higher wages than technicians in smaller cities or counties. States are divided into small sections called counties.

Salary

Crime lab technicians in the United States earn between $15,500 and $49,500 per year (all figures late 1990s). The average income is around $28,000 per year. Many crime lab technicians work for cities or counties. State governments and the U.S. government also employ crime lab technicians.

Crime lab technicians can work for local, state, and national governments.

Canadian crime lab technicians earn between about $32,000 and $58,000 per year. The average salary for crime lab technicians is between $39,361 and $47,885. Salaries vary according to training and experience.

Crime lab technicians who earn bachelor's degrees receive higher wages. These crime lab technicians also are called crime lab scientists or forensic scientists.

Benefits
Crime lab technicians usually receive salaries and benefits from their employers. Benefits are payments or services in addition to salaries or wages. They include insurance, retirement plans, and paid sick and vacation time.

Job Outlook
People with the right training and experience will be able to find jobs as crime lab technicians. In the United States, the profession is expected to

Crime lab technicians' salaries depend on their education and experience.

have average growth. In Canada, the profession is expected to have fair growth. The RCMP employs more forensic specialists than forensic technologists. There are fewer technologist jobs available in Canada.

Chapter 5

Where the Job Can Lead

Crime lab technicians can advance in several ways. Most advance as they gain experience and education. Increased experience and education can lead to jobs with greater responsibilities and higher salaries. Other technicians can advance by moving into jobs in related career fields.

Advancing on the Job

Job advancement for crime lab technicians is closely linked to education. Technicians who have associate's degrees often go back to school. They earn bachelor's degrees. Many of these crime lab technicians then go on to earn master's degrees.

Many crime lab technicians go back to school for advanced training.

People earn master's degrees by completing advanced courses of study at colleges or universities. People usually earn master's degrees in two years.

Crime lab technicians can take special classes related to their jobs. For example, technicians may learn to work with special photographic equipment. They also may learn special ways of identifying fingerprints. These extra skills can help technicians advance in their jobs.

Advancing in the Profession

Some crime lab technicians become managers or supervisors. These people oversee other technicians. Managers and supervisors earn higher salaries than less experienced technicians.

Experienced crime lab technicians can become crime lab directors. Directors are responsible for the work done at the labs. Some crime lab directors can advance to jobs as directors of

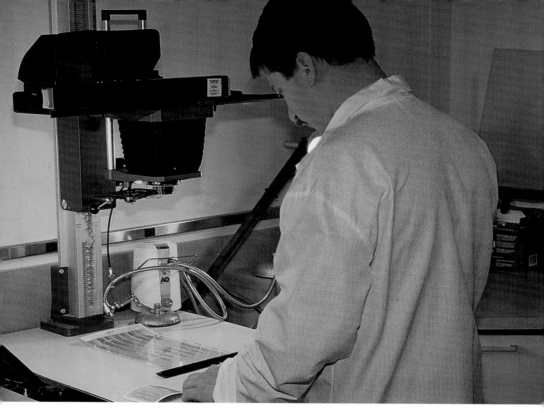

Crime lab technicians can take special classes related to their jobs.

larger labs. They can become state crime lab directors. These individuals decide how labs in a certain state operate.

Technicians can work in a variety of laboratories.

Related Careers

Crime lab technicians usually have interests in law enforcement, science, and medical technology. Other career areas involve similar interests. For example, a person interested in law enforcement could pursue a career as a police officer or detective.

Careers in science or medical technology include work in other kinds of laboratories. Medical lab technicians do work similar to the work of crime lab technicians. They must follow many of the same procedures. Their education also is similar. But medical lab technicians work at labs in hospitals and clinics. They also may work in labs that process medical lab tests.

Lab technicians also may work for companies. Technicians at some manufacturing companies help develop products. For example, technicians may work for companies that make new medicines. They also can work for companies that develop other products. These products include cleaners, makeup, glues, or plastics. Technicians may need bachelor's degrees in chemistry or other science areas to work at these companies.

Words to Know

chemistry (KEM-is-tree)—the scientific study of substances, what they are composed of, and the ways they react with each other

crime scene (KRIME SEEN)—the place where something happened that was against the law

DNA (dee en AY)—the molecule that carries the genetic code that gives living things their special physical features

evidence (EV-uh-duhnss)—information, items, and facts that help prove something is true or false; crime lab technicians gather and test evidence found at crime and accident scenes.

suspect (SUHSS-pekt)—someone thought to be responsible for a crime

testify (TESS-tuh-fye)—to state facts in court

toxicology (tok-si-KOL-uh-jee)—the scientific study of drugs and poisons

trace evidence (TRAYSS EV-uh-duhnss)—tiny pieces of evidence such as a hair, cloth fibers, or powder

victim (VIK-tuhm)—a person who is hurt, killed, or made to suffer because of an accident or crime

To Learn More

Evans, Colin. *The Casebook of Forensic Detection: How Science Solved 100 of the World's Most Baffling Crimes*. New York: Wiley, 1996.

Fisher, David. *Hard Evidence: How Detectives inside the FBI's Sci-Crime Lab Have Helped Solve America's Toughest Cases*. New York: Simon & Schuster, 1995.

Sheely, Robert. *Police Lab: Using Science to Solve Crimes*. New York: Silver Moon Press, 1993.

Zonderman, Jon. *Beyond the Crime Lab: The New Science of Investigation*. New York: John Wiley, 1998.

Useful Addresses

American Academy of Forensic Sciences
P.O. Box 669
Colorado Springs, CO 80901-0669

Canadian Society of Forensic Science
2660 Southvale Crescent
Suite 215
Ottawa, ON K1B 4W5
Canada

Federal Bureau of Investigation
J. Edgar Hoover F.B.I. Building
935 Pennsylvania Avenue NW
Washington, DC 20535-0001

Internet Sites

American Academy of Forensic Sciences
http://www.aafs.org

American Board of Criminalistics
http://www.criminalistics.com/ABC

Canadian Society of Forensic Science
http://www.csfs.ca/index.htm

FBI Kid's and Youth Educational Page
http://www.fbi.gov/kids/kids.htm

Justice for Kids and Youth
http://www.usdoj.gov/kidspage

Index